DESIGN and MAKE

Wheels and Transport

John Williams

WAYLAND

DESIGN and MAKE

Houses and Homes
Things to Wear
Toys and Games
Wheels and Transport
Simple Machines
Water Projects

First published in 1997 by Wayland Publishers Ltd,
61 Western Road, Hove, East Sussex BN3 1JD, England
© Copyright 1997 Wayland Publishers Ltd
Series planned and produced by Margot Richardson
Find Wayland on the internet at http: //www.wayland.co.uk

British Library Cataloguing in Publication Data
Williams, John, 1936–
Wheels and transport. - (Design & make)
1. Vehicles - Design and construction - Juvenile literature
I. Title
629.2'31

ISBN 0 7502 2077 5

Commissioned photography by Zul Mukhida
Designed by Tim Mayer
Edited by Margot Richardson
Equipment supplied by Technology Teaching Systems Ltd, Alfreton, UK
Printed and bound in Italy by G. Canale & C.S.p.A., Turin

CONTENTS

INTRODUCTION

From bicycles to jumbo jets, almost all types of transport use wheels. Wheels let people move heavy loads over land. Although a load can be dragged along the ground, putting wheels underneath makes moving it much easier.

To move big things before wheels were invented, people put round poles underneath them. The large stones used to build the pyramids in Egypt, and Stonehenge in England, were probably rolled along in this way.

The first wheels were made of solid wood. Later, spokes were invented, and metal took the place of wood. Rubber tyres were used as long ago as 1845 but they did not work well at first.

Vehicles need to be designed for the types of load that they have to carry. The designs for a garden wheelbarrow or a double-decker bus are very different, but each one is ideal for the jobs it has to do.

There are many different types of vehicles that have wheels. Some are pulled along by animals such as horses, or by people. Others have petrol engines, but engines can also work with electricity and even gas. Not all vehicles have four wheels. How many different types can you see in this street in India?

A monorail is a type of electric train. Instead of running on two tracks with wheels on either side, it runs on one central track. Some monorail trains do not need a driver. They are controlled by a computer instead.

For hundreds of years, all vehicles were made mainly of wood and were pulled by horses. When steam and petrol engines were developed, the designs of vehicles began to change.

Technology has helped to make modern vehicles safer and more comfortable. However, more and more people own cars, and trucks are becoming larger all the time. The fumes and noise from their engines can cause pollution. People who design and make these vehicles will have to solve these problems in the future.

Most modern bicycles now have light frames and many gears. But the basic design of the bicycle has changed very little since it was first given two equal sized wheels.

WOBBLY WHEELS

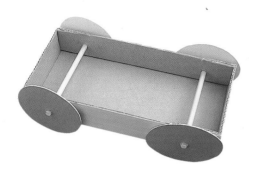

What happens when wheels are not round? Here is a simple cart to make with oval wheels.

Wheels are usually attached to rods or tubes, called axles. Axles are made from wood or metal. They can be very short with just one wheel on them, such as at the front of a wheelbarrow or on a tricycle. Other axles are longer, and have a wheel at each end.

YOU WILL NEED

- A shallow box, or box lid
- Two pieces of 5mm-diameter dowel, 1cm longer than the width of the box
- Four round wheels made from thick card, with 5mm centre holes
- Hole punch
- Junior hacksaw
- PVA glue
- Pencil
- Ruler
- Scissors
- Plank of wood

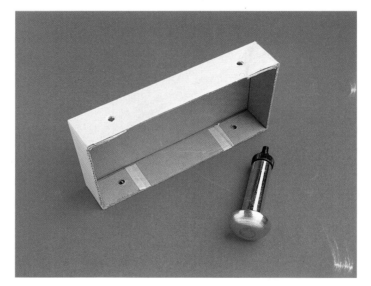

1 Punch two holes in the sides of one end of the box. They should be exactly opposite each other. Punch two more holes at the other end.

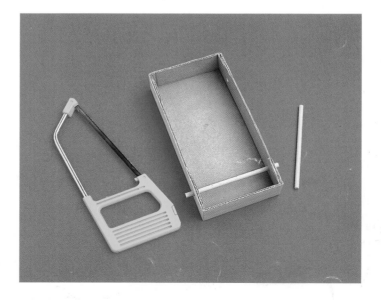

2 Cut the dowel so that each piece is just 1cm longer than the width of the box. Slide the dowels through the holes. They should turn easily.

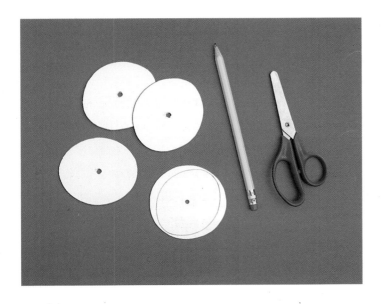

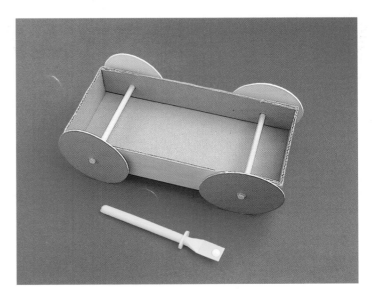

3 Draw an oval on one of the round wheels. Cut out the oval shape. Use this as a template to make each wheel the same size and shape.

4 Push a wheel on to each end of the dowels. Make sure each pair is pointing the same way. Put a little glue onto each wheel to fix it to the axle.

5 Make a steep slope with a plank of wood. Run your cart down the slope. What happens with the oval wheels?

NOW TRY THIS

Change the oval wheels for different sized pairs of round wheels. Keep the small wheels on one side and large wheels on the other. What happens?

HOVERCRAFT

A craft knife can be dangerous if it is not used properly. Always ask an adult to help you use one.

- **To avoid accidents, never play with sharp knives**
- **Always use a steel rule to guide the knife**

YOU WILL NEED

- Polystyrene ceiling tile
- Short cardboard tube, approx 3cm diameter
- Tissue paper
- PVA glue
- Steel rule
- Craft knife
- Pencil
- Ruler
- Scissors
- Hair dryer (optional)

A hovercraft is almost the only form of land transport that does not need wheels. Instead, it is held up by a powerful jet of air that is pushed downwards, against the land or the sea. This cushion of air allows the hovercraft to move easily in any direction.

Hovercraft are used to travel across water. This large one can transport many cars and hundreds of people.

1 Mark a square on the polystyrene tile. Each side should be between 15 and 20cm long. Carefully cut the square using the craft knife and a steel rule.

2 Hold the cardboard tube in the centre of the polystyrene and draw round it. Ask an adult to cut a round hole, using the craft knife. Put a little glue on the end of the tube and push it into the tile. Let the glue dry.

3 Cut a long piece of tissue paper for the hovercraft's skirt. It should be long enough to go all the way round the tile, plus 2cm, and be about 4cm wide.

4 Glue the paper skirt right round the side edge of the tile. Where the ends meet, let them overlap and glue them together. Let the glue dry.

5 Blow down the tube, or use a hairdryer to make a current of air. What happens to the polystyrene tile?

NOW TRY THIS

Try changing the design of the hovercraft. Make the tile bigger or smaller, and the skirt longer or shorter. What is the size that makes it work best?

ROMAN CHARIOT

YOU WILL NEED

- Corrugated plastic, 5mm thick
- Wooden dowel, 5mm diameter
- Two wooden wheels, approx 5cm diameter, 5mm thick, with 5mm centre holes
- Two cardboard circles, approx 2.5cm diameter, with 5mm centre holes
- Small pieces PVC tubing, approx 5mm diameter and 5mm long
- Metal paper fasteners
- Cardboard/felt/string/pipe cleaners/tissue paper
- Rubber bands
- Masking tape
- Junior hacksaw
- Pencil
- Ruler
- Scissors

The ancient Romans lived before cars, trains or even bicycles were invented. They used horses to pull chariots which carried one or two people. Because the chariots were small and light, they could move quite quickly.

1 Cut out a rectangle of corrugated plastic, about 10cm x 8cm, with the lines in the plastic running in the same direction as the long sides.

2 Cut a piece of dowel about 2cm longer than the long side. Push it through the plastic in the centre to make a fixed axle.

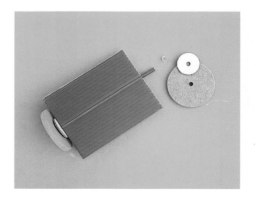

3 Put the wheels on each end of the dowel. Add the small card circles first, then the wooden wheels. Hold the wheels on with the small pieces of PVC tubing.

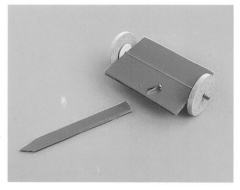

4 Cut a long narrow piece of plastic to make the pulling shaft. It should be about 14cm long. Join it to the rectangle, in the middle, with a metal paper fastener.

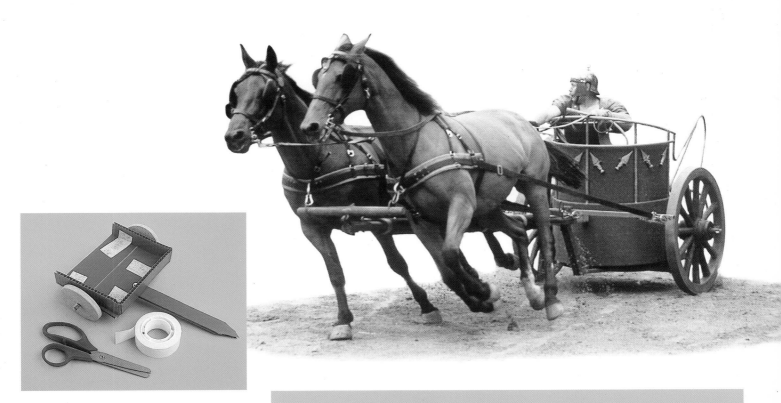

5 Cut out a narrow piece of plastic to go round three sides of the rectangle. Bend it where it will go round the corners. Join it to the rectangle with masking tape.

Roman chariots could go quite fast. They did not weigh very much, and usually only carried one or two people. As well as using them to get from one place to another, the Romans held chariot races. This is a modern chariot, made in the same way as the Roman ones.

6 Make two model horses to look as though they are pulling the chariot. Try using cardboard, felt, string, pipe cleaners and tissue paper. Also make some 'animal skins' to line the chariot.

JET-POWERED CAR

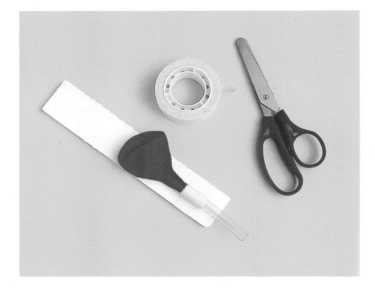

1 Cut the lip from the balloon. Put the plastic tube into the mouth of the balloon. Pull the end tightly round the tube and fix it on with masking tape. Make sure no air can escape.

2 Using the craft knife and steel rule, cut a piece of polystyrene tile about 16cm long and 3cm wide. Fix the balloon with masking tape so that the tube is at one end.

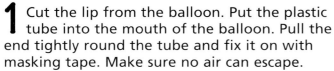

YOU WILL NEED

- Polystyrene ceiling tile
- Balloon
- Flexible PVC tubing, about 6cm long
- Mapping pins (with large heads)
- Cardboard
- Masking tape
- Craft knife
- Steel rule
- Pencil
- Scissors

Jet engines are sometimes used for special racing cars. They give a strong, large push so the car will go very fast. The air from a balloon will move a model car, but the car must be very light and simple.

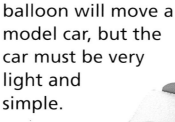

A craft knife can be dangerous if it is not used properly. Always ask an adult to help you use one.

- **Always use a steel rule to guide the knife.**

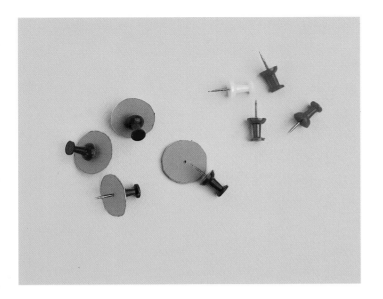

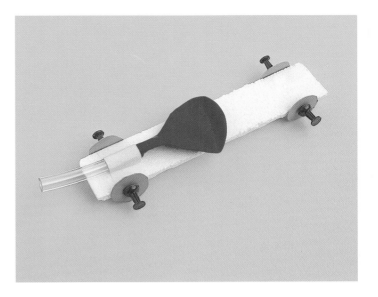

3 Cut out four cardboard wheels about 2cm in diameter. Push a mapping pin through the centre of each wheel. Make sure that the wheels can move freely on the pins.

4 Push the pins into the sides of the tile, 2cm from each end. Leave just enough of the pins sticking out for the wheels to turn.

5 Blow up the balloon. Keep your finger over the mouth of the tube. Put the buggy on a very smooth surface, and let go.

A jet ski has an engine that pushes out strong jets of water. They make the ski move very fast over water, but the ground is too hard and bumpy for them to work on land.

NOW TRY THIS

Design an even smaller car. Will a bigger balloon make any difference?

MOON BUGGY

YOU WILL NEED

- Thick cardboard
- Two plastic drinking straws, approx 6mm diameter
- Wooden dowel, approx 5mm diameter
- Eight circles of thick card for wheels, approx 6cm diameter, with centre holes to match the dowel
- Corrugated cardboard for wheels
- Masking tape
- PVA glue
- Hole punch
- Pencil
- Ruler
- Scissors
- Junior hacksaw

When men landed on the moon in the 1970s, they took with them some special vehicles. Obviously, there are no roads on the moon. One of the main problems with driving there were the many loose rocks, so their electric buggies were built with large knobbly wheels to grip the ground.

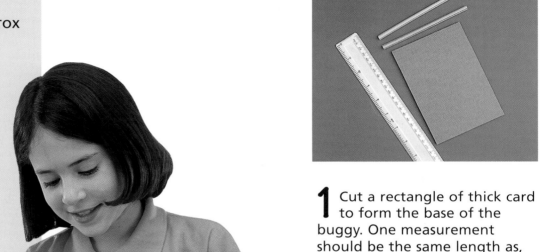

1 Cut a rectangle of thick card to form the base of the buggy. One measurement should be the same length as, or shorter than, the straws.

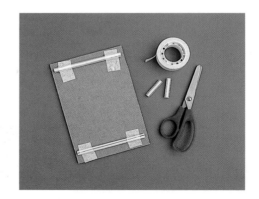

2 Using masking tape, stick a straw near each shorter end of the card. They should be about 1cm in from the edge of the card, and exactly parallel to the edge.

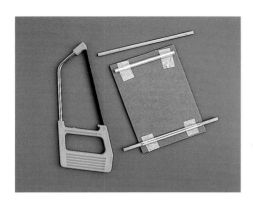  

3 Cut two lengths of dowel for the axles. They should be 5cm longer than the short side of the cardboard rectangle. Push the dowel through the straws. The axles should be able to move freely.

4 Cut four strips of corrugated card 2cm wide and long enough to fit round the edges of the wheels. Glue the edges of the card to a pair of discs to make four wide wheels.

5 Push the wheels on to each end of the dowel. Fix the wheels on to the dowel with a little glue.

NOW TRY THIS

You will need to design what to put on the top of this chassis. Make some drawings showing special seats for the astronauts, radio antennae and even a flag. Make these out of cardboard and fix them to the chassis.

The moon vehicles were called Lunar Rovers. They let the astronauts explore much further from the landing sites than was possible on earlier missions. The cars had to be left behind; they are still on the moon.

CABLE CAR AND LIFTS

YOU WILL NEED

- Two small blocks of wood
- Two cup hooks
- Two G clamps
- Rubber bands
- Thick fishing line
- Three small boxes
- Paper clips
- Two cotton reels
- Thin wire and wire cutters or pipe cleaners
- Cardboard
- Weight, such as modelling clay, or small toy
- PVA glue
- Masking tape
- Cotton thread
- Scissors

These kinds of transport do not have wheels that move along the ground. They hang from thick wires, and are pulled by cables or ropes. They need special wheels called pulleys, over which the cables or ropes have to move. The pulleys may be attached to the car, or at each end of the cable.

Cable cars are often used to take people up to the top of mountains. On the way, the passengers have a wonderful view of the mountain scenery. This cable car is in Switzerland. It can carry more than 40 people at one time.

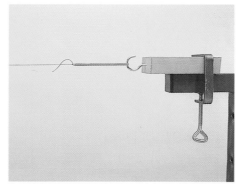

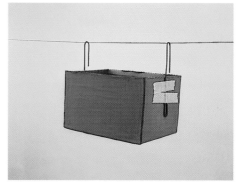

1 You need to fix the ends of the cable firmly. Screw the cup hooks into two small blocks of wood. Fix the blocks tightly to two tables with G clamps. Ask an adult to help you.

2 Cut a piece of fishing line. Tie a rubber band to each end of the line. Put one rubber band over each of the cup hooks so that the bands stretch and keep the line taut.

3 Straighten out two paper clips, leaving one bend at each end. Use masking tape to fix the clips to opposite ends of a box. Use the hooked ends to hang the box on the line.

NOW TRY THIS

- **See how much load you can carry in the cable car.**

- **Send messages from one end of the room to the other.**

- **Can you design and make a cable car that goes uphill?**

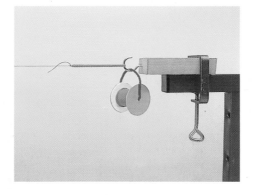

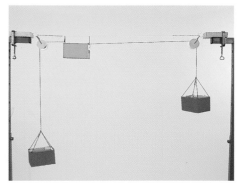

4 Cut four circles of card, about 2cm wider than the ends of the cotton reels. Glue the circles on each end of the reels and let the glue dry. Cut two pieces of wire or take two pipe cleaners. Use them to hang the cotton reels from the hooks.

5 Fix some thread to each end of the box. Pass the ends over the cotton reels. Fix the free ends of the threads to the other boxes so that they hang below the cotton reels. Make sure that there is enough thread to pull the cable car the complete length of the fishing line.

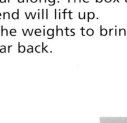

6 Put a weight in one box so that as it falls it pulls the cable car along. The box at the other end will lift up. Exchange the weights to bring the cable car back.

RAIL CAR AND TRACKS

Trains and trams, which run on rails, need to have special wheels with metal lips, called flanges. These keep the train on the rails. The flanges go on the insides of the rails.

YOU WILL NEED

- Small cardboard box
- Two pieces of 5mm dowel, 2cm longer than the width of the box
- Four round wheels made from thick card, about 4cm diameter, with centre holes to match the dowel
- Four wooden wheels, approx 3cm diameter, 5mm thick, with centre holes to match the dowel
- Wood, approx 1 x 1cm square: two long lengths
- Thin card (for roof)
- Hole punch
- PVA glue
- Pencil
- Ruler
- Scissors
- Paint and paintbrush

1 Punch four holes in the sides of the box, about 2cm from each end. Make sure that they are exactly opposite each other, and about 1cm from the bottom of the box.

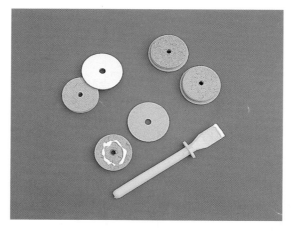

2 Glue one thick wooden wheel onto each of the larger thin cardboard wheels. Make sure the holes in the centre overlap exactly. The thin wheel will form the flange.

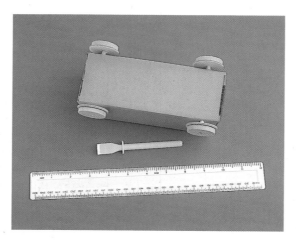

3 Push the dowel axles through the holes in the box. Glue a wheel on to each end so that the flange is on the inside. Make sure the wheels are straight. Each pair must be the same distance apart.

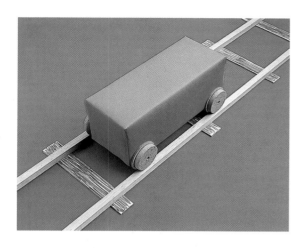

4 Use long lengths of the 1 x 1cm wood for the rails. Stick them to pieces of card. They should be the same distance apart as the wheels.

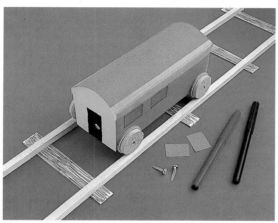

5 Decorate the rail car and add the windows and doors. Make a roof with a curved piece of thin card.

NOW TRY THIS

Fix a small electric motor (1.5V–4.5V) in the centre of one end of the tracks. Wire it up to a battery (4.5V minimum). Stick a piece of cotton thread to the front of the rail car. Tie the other end of the thread to the spindle of the electric motor. The motor will pull the car along the track.

Most modern trains get their power from electricity, or sometimes from diesel fuel. This is an older steam engine in China.

CARRIAGE WITH SUSPENSION

YOU WILL NEED

- Small cardboard box, about 10 x 14cm
- Wood, approx 1 x 1cm square
- Two thick cardboard triangles, each side about 3cm long
- Four round wheels made from thick card, about 5cm diameter
- Four mapping pins
- Thin wire, such as plastic-covered garden wire
- Masking tape
- PVA glue
- Junior hacksaw
- Pencil
- Ruler
- Scissors
- Paints and paintbrush

There are many different kinds of spring mechanisms on modern vehicles. They are all designed to protect the vehicle and its passengers from damage when they are travelling over rough ground. Modern suspension systems can be a complicated collection of springs and levers, but many years ago only a bendy piece of metal or even wood was all that was used.

Carriages pulled by horses carried goods and passengers. This is an artist's picture of a mail coach, nearly 200 years ago. The man at the back is throwing down a mail bag to the person on the ground. The passengers travelled inside as well as on top of the carriage.

1 Cut two pieces of wood a little wider than the box. Cut one piece the same size as the length of the box.

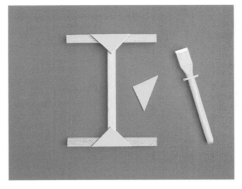

2 Put a little glue on each end of the long piece of wood, and join it to the centre of each of the short pieces. For added strength, glue on the two cardboard triangles over each join.

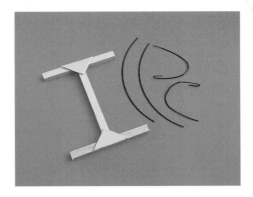

3 Cut four short lengths of the garden wire. Make a small loop in one end of each piece. Bend each piece into a shape like a flattened C.

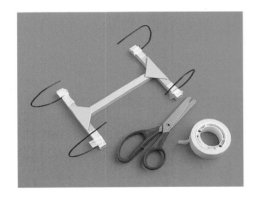

4 Using masking tape, attach each piece of wire to the wooden frame. The looped end of the wire should be stuck to the wood, about 5mm in from the wheel. Stick the other ends of the wire to the underside of the box.

5 Join the wheels on to the frame with mapping pins. Push a pin through the centre of each wheel. Make sure each wheel can turn freely.

6 Decorate your box to look like an old horse-drawn carriage. It should have windows and doors on each side.

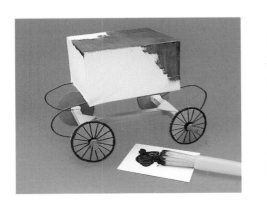

TROLLEY WITH STEERING HANDLE

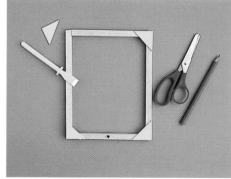

YOU WILL NEED

- Wood, approx 1 x 1cm square: two pieces 18cm long, three pieces 12cm long

- Wooden dowel, 5mm diameter: two pieces 17cm long

- Wooden dowel, 5mm diameter: two pieces 3cm long (for handle)

- Small piece of thick card

- Four circles of thick card for wheels, approx 4cm diameter, with centre holes to match the dowel

- PVA glue

- Junior drill with 5mm drill bit

- Needle file (optional)

- Hole punch

- Pencil

- Ruler

- Scissors

Vehicles need ways of steering, to help them go round corners. The front wheels of modern cars and lorries can move to the left or to the right, but with old-fashioned carts and trolleys it was often just the shafts and handles that turned.

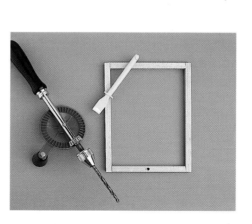

1 Drill a hole through the centre of a 12cm length of wood. This piece will be the front part of the chassis. Glue this piece, another 12cm length, and the two 18cm lengths together to make a frame.

2 Lay the frame flat on the table. Cut four triangles of card with two sides 3cm long and a base 4.5cm long. Glue the 3cm sides of the cardboard triangles to each corner of the wooden frame.

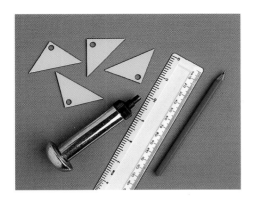

3 Cut four more triangles with two sides about 4cm long and a longest side of 5cm. Punch holes near the points made by the shorter sides. Make sure they are all in the same place on each triangle

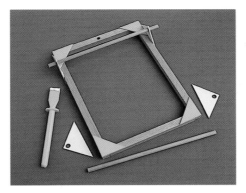

4 Stick the triangles to the sides at each end of the long pieces of wood. Make sure each pair of triangles is exactly opposite each other, and pass the long pieces of dowel through the holes.

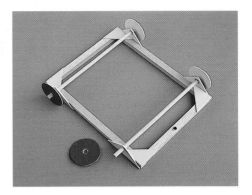

5 The dowel should turn easily. Glue a card wheel to the ends of each dowel axle. Make sure each wheel is straight.

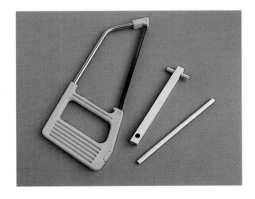

6 Drill two holes in the last piece of wood. Make one hole about 1cm from the end, the other in the same place at the other end, but through the opposite sides of the wood. Tap a short, 3cm piece of dowel right through this hole to make a pulling handle.

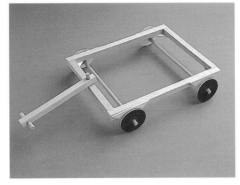

7 Tap the last 3cm piece of dowel into the hole on the trolley frame. Put the handle on the trolley. You may need to use a needle file to make this hole in the handle bigger, so that the handle can move from side to side.

NOW TRY THIS

Glue a piece of card onto the top of the chassis. Design and make a top for your trolley. It could be a flower seller's barrow or perhaps a covered wagon.

Modern lorries steer in the same way as the trolley on these pages. The front section of the lorry can turn to the right or left. The back section follows on in the direction it is pulled.

GRAVITY VEHICLE

YOU WILL NEED

- Lid of a shoe box
- Wooden dowel for axles, 5mm diameter: two pieces about 2cm longer than the width of the box
- Wooden dowel, 5mm diameter: two pieces about 30cm long, one piece 10cm long
- Four circles of thick card for wheels, approx 5cm diameter, with centre holes to match the dowel
- Cotton thread
- Plastic modelling clay (eg Plasticine)
- PVA glue
- Masking tape
- Hole punch
- Ruler

Before petrol engines were invented, many different methods were tried to make vehicles move. Apart from steam engines, nothing worked as well as a horse. However, some people experimented with the energy of a falling weight.

1 Punch two pairs of holes in the sides of the box lid, 2cm in from each end. Slide the dowel axles through the holes. Make sure they turn easily. Glue the wheels onto the ends of the axles.

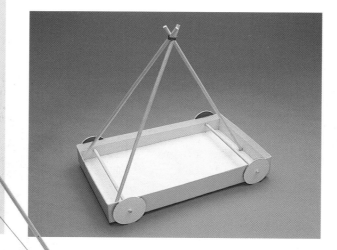

2 Glue the long pieces of dowel into the box lid, to form a pyramid. Two pieces should be at the front corners, and the third halfway along the back. Fix them at the top with cotton and glue.

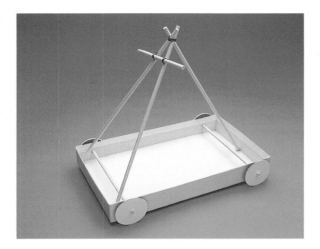

3 Tie the last piece of dowel across the front of the pyramid. Glue it as well. Attach it as near to the top as possible.

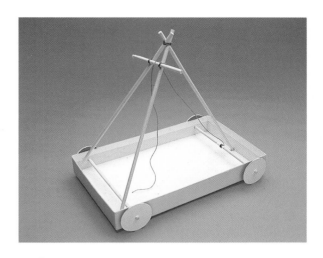

4 Cut a long piece of cotton thread. Stick one end to the rear axle and pass the other end over the dowel at the top of the pyramid.

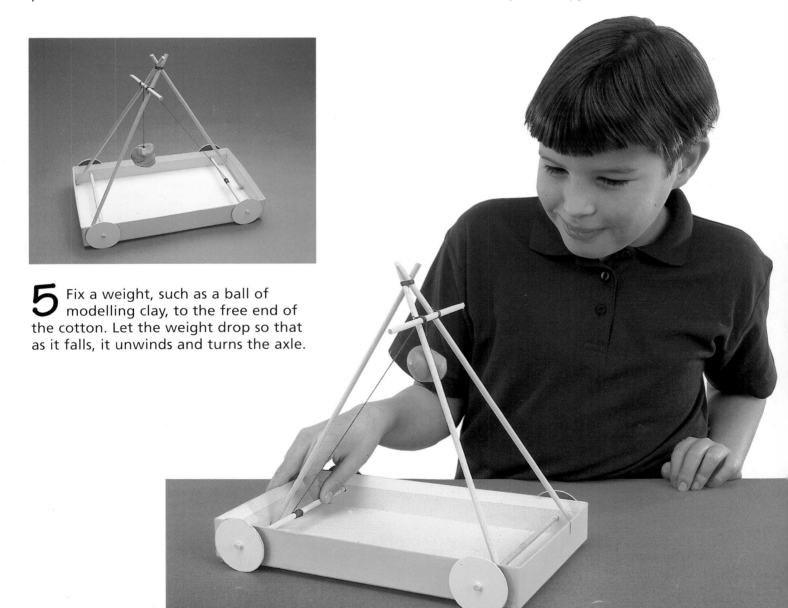

5 Fix a weight, such as a ball of modelling clay, to the free end of the cotton. Let the weight drop so that as it falls, it unwinds and turns the axle.

LAND YACHT

YOU WILL NEED

- Cardboard box, such as a shoe box
- Wood, approx 1 x 1cm square: two pieces about 16cm longer than the length of the box
- Wooden dowel for axles, 5mm diameter: two pieces 14cm longer than the width of the box
- Wooden dowel, 5mm diameter: one piece for the mast (length depends on size of box)
- Four cotton reels
- Four spring clothes pegs
- Four small pieces PVC tubing, approx 5mm diameter and 5mm long
- Tissue paper
- Cotton thread
- PVA glue
- Masking tape
- Scissors

All things need energy to make them move. Petrol provides the energy for most cars and lorries. Other vehicles use electricity. It is even possible to use the energy of the wind to move them along.

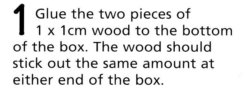

1 Glue the two pieces of 1 x 1cm wood to the bottom of the box. The wood should stick out the same amount at either end of the box.

2 Fix the spring clothes pegs onto the ends of the wood, using masking tape. Clip the dowel axles into each pair of pegs.

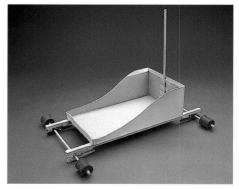

3 Slide a cotton reel onto each end of the axles. Put the plastic tube on each end of the dowel to keep the reels on. The reels should run freely on the dowel axles.

4 Cut the two long sides of the box to give it a streamlined shape. Fix the dowel mast inside the box, in the centre, using the masking tape.

Sand yachting is a sport like sailing on water. A lightweight buggy is pushed along by the wind on a sail. A smooth land surface is needed, so the sand yachts use flat, sandy beaches.

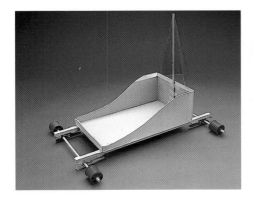

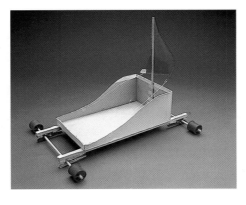

NOW TRY THIS

Design a different sail for your yacht. Try one with a boom, like a real sailing boat, or a set of sails like old square-rigged sailing ships.

5 Cut a large triangle of tissue paper for the sail. Glue the top corner of the paper to the top of the mast, so that the sail hangs down in front of the mast.

6 Use masking tape to fix cotton thread to each bottom corner of the sail. Stick the other ends of the thread to the back edge of the box. The yacht is now ready to move.

ELECTRIC BUGGY

YOU WILL NEED

- Two empty plastic drink bottles
- Wood, approx 1 x 1cm square: two pieces about 30–40cm long, depending on the size of the bottles
- Wooden dowel, approx 5mm diameter: two pieces 6cm longer than the bottles
- Balsa wood: one piece approx 5mm thick, 8cm wide and the same length as the dowel
- Four spring clothes pegs
- Small electric motor (1.5–4.5V)
- Battery (4.5V minimum)
- Single core electric wire
- Rubber bands (various sizes)
- Masking tape
- Wire cutters
- Scissors

Some cars can be powered by electricity. They are clean and quiet. However, they are still at an early stage of development. In the future they will work better, but at the moment they have little power, and their batteries need to be recharged every few kilometres.

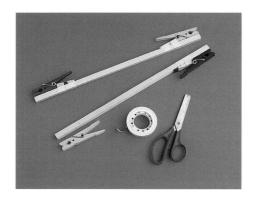

1 Using masking tape, fix a clothes peg to each end of the 1 x 1cm wood.

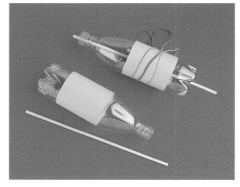

2 Make a hole in the bottom of each bottle. Put the dowel through the hole and out of the top of each bottle. Put three or four different-sized rubber bands round one of the bottles.

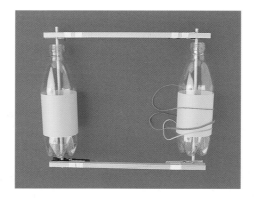

3 Clip each end of the dowel into the clothes pegs. The bottles should run freely but the axles should not move. If necessary, wrap some masking tape round the dowel to make it bigger.

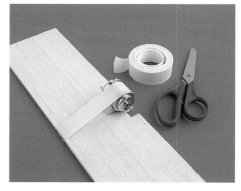

4 Cut a 1 x 1cm notch out of the edge of the balsa wood. Fix the motor firmly to the wood with masking tape. The spindle should be over the notch.

Electric cars do not make much noise and do not give off fumes. They are ideal for use in towns and cities. Many car companies are working on electric cars, such as this one, for the future.

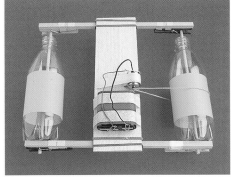

5 Use rubber bands to fix the balsa wood across the middle of the wood lengths, so that the motor faces the bottle which has the other rubber bands on it. Pull one of them over the spindle. Make sure it is not too tight.

6 Tape the battery to the wood next to the motor. Cut two wires and fix them to the lugs at the back of the motor. Put paper clips on the other ends of the wires so they can hold on to the battery terminals.

NOW TRY THIS

● Design and make a switch for the motor.
This needs to have two metal parts that can be put together and taken apart, such as two paper fasteners in a piece of cardboard. If you then make the wires long enough, you can walk alongside the buggy, holding the switch. This will make the buggy stop and start.

● Design and make a body to go over the buggy you have just made.

GLOSSARY

axle A wood or metal rod on which a wheel turns.

boom A pole on a ship. The sail is attached to it, and it has one end fixed to the mast.

cable A strong metal wire, used for electricity or to pull heavy loads.

chassis The main frame of a vehicle, including axles and wheels. The body is fixed on to it.

coach Another name for a carriage, such as a horse-drawn or a train carriage.

diameter The distance across the centre of a circle, from one side to the other.

diesel A type of petrol, used to drive engines.

fumes Air or smoke that smells bad.

gravity The pull of the earth that makes things fall to the ground when they are dropped.

jet The push of air from an engine or water from a hose. Both these forces can be used to drive machines.

load The weight raised or lowered by a machine, or carried by a vehicle or animal.

passenger A person who travels in a vehicle, boat or aircraft.

pollution Dirt in the air or on the land, such as smoke from cars or chemicals from factories.

pulley A special wheel around which a rope is pulled to raise a weight or move an object.

recharged When a battery is given more electricity for it to continue working.

shaft A straight wooden pole fixed to the front of a cart.

spoke A wooden bar or metal rod on a wheel. It is fixed from the centre to the rim.

springs Curved or bent pieces of metal.

streamlined The special shape of the body of a vehicle, boat or aeroplane to help it go faster.

suspension Springs and levers fixed to the axles of a vehicle. These let the body move smoothly when the vehicle is moving over rough ground. This gives the passengers a more comfortable ride.

switch A way of turning things such as lights or motors off and on by opening or closing the electric circuit.

template A shape used to mark and cut out a number of the same shapes.

vehicle Anything which carries people or goods over land or through space.

yacht A boat or vehicle that is pushed along by the wind.

BOOKS TO READ

Exploring Technology: Land Transport by Malcolm Dixon, Wayland, 1991

Eyewitness Guides: Train by John Coiley, Dorling Kindersley, 1992

How Things Work: Wheels at Work by Andrew Dunn, Wayland, 1992

Look Into the Past: The Romans by Peter Hicks, Wayland, 1993

Timelines: Transport by David Salariya, Franklin Watts, 1992

Transport: a Visual History by Anthony Wilson, Dorling Kindersley, 1995

Transport by Design by Ian Graham, Simon & Schuster Young Books, 1994

The World's Transport: Road Travel by Tim Wood, Wayland, 1992

TEACHERS' NOTES

Wobbly Wheels Making this simple design introduces children to the basic skills of measurement, cutting and sawing. The axles must be properly in place, and the wood to be cut should be held securely in a bench-hook or vice. Using irregular shaped wheels is fun, but it emphasises the need for accuracy in design.

Hovercraft This model is designed to show the scientific principles involved. It is very important to reduce the weight to the minimum, and that no air can escape from under the tissue-paper 'skirt'. Children should be encouraged to design more complex models, incorporating some motive power. It is possible to build a model with a rubber-band-powered propeller which not only pulls it along, but also drives air down a scoop. This air produces the lifting force.

Roman Chariot This simple model introduces children to new materials, and to the idea of a fixed axle on which only the wheels themselves revolve. There is scope for further design. Children can make model horses, charioteers, or add detail to the chariot itself, all based on accurate historical references.

Jet-Powered Car This model illustrates the importance of power to weight ratios. What power there is when air is expelled from a balloon is short lived. The vehicle must be very light if it is to move at all, and there must be as little friction as possible between the wheels and axles.

Moon Buggy This model is based on a simple chassis. Plastic straws must be attached to the card base with masking tape as there is no suitable glue for children of this age. PVA glue can be used to make the wheels and to stick anything to the top of the chassis. Children should be encouraged to make careful designs for the top of the chassis incorporating appropriate objects.

Cable Car and Lifts This model uses simple pulley wheels. Children of this age do not need to know the principles involved in using a block and tackle to lift a heavy weight. However, they can be introduced to the idea of a pulley as a method of facilitating movement. In this case, it allows a weight to be used as the driving force to move the car. Counter-weights of this kind can be found in some funicular railways, and often the weight used is water. The cable must be tight, and there should be minimum friction between the cable and the car. Children should be encouraged to think of other driving mechanisms, such as rubber-band-powered propellers, and jet-propelled balloons.

Rail Car and Tracks This model introduces children to the importance of special wheels for rail tracks. There is plenty of scope for design work, both for the model and for the layout of the track. If an electric motor and cable is used to pull the car, children can also design a signalling system to go with it.

Carriage with Suspension Although this model is made within an historical context, it introduces children to the modern idea of a chassis equipped with some form of spring. Modern suspensions are often a combination of levers and springs, but can sometimes be made from rubber air cushions.

Trolley with Steering Handle Children will need to be shown how to use a small hand drill, and can practise drilling holes in a spare piece of wood which should be fixed to the bench with a G-clamp. If low temperature glue-guns are used to stick the pieces together it should be realised that this can only be a temporary fixture. It is only when the card triangles are glued on with PVA that the model can be moved.

Gravity Vehicle The idea for this kind of vehicle was first considered by Hero in the second century BC. He understood its limitations and so used it for self-moving scenery in his automata theatres. Used for this purpose, the vehicles only had to move very short distances. It is very important that friction is reduced to a minimum. Children should be encouraged to consider the forces at work on such a vehicle: gravity and friction.

Land Yacht Wind power has been used for land transport since the early Chinese first put sails on barrows to help them carry heavy loads. A wind-powered vehicle was designed by Roberto Valturio in Italy during the 15th century, and a rail car equipped with a sail was built in the 19th century. Children can design different sail rigs and experiment with the relationship between sail area and wind strength.

Electric Buggy Electricity is a form of energy, and can be used to drive a variety of vehicles. The pegs can be used on many designs to hold axles, and are convenient for changing wheel systems. Make sure that the rubber band is at the correct tension. Children should be encouraged to consider that the relative circumferences of the motor spindle and the connected plastic bottle make a rudimentary gearing system. They can also reverse the polarity of the battery to make the buggy go backwards. This can be incorporated into their designs for a switch.

INDEX

Acknowledgements

The author and publishers wish to thank the following for their kind assistance with this book: models Josie Kearns, Yasmin Mukhida, Charlotte Page, Tom Rigby and Ranga Silva. Also Gabriella Casemore, Zul Mukhida, Philippa Smith and Gus Ferguson.

For the use of their library photographs, grateful thanks are due to: Eye Ubiquitous p8 (R Battersby), p13 (Darren Maybury), p16 (H. Rooney), p23 (David Gurr); James Davis Travel Photography, p5 top;Topham Picturepoint p11, p15, p27, p29 (Citroen).
All other photographs belong to the Wayland Picture Library: p4 (Jimmy Holmes), p5 right (APM Studio), p19 (Julia Waterlow), p20.